Rosary for the Holy Souls in Purgatory

The
Rosary for the
Holy Souls
in Purgatory

Susan Tassone

Our Sunday Visitor Publishing Division
Our Sunday Visitor, Inc.
Huntington, Indiana 46750

With Ecclesiastical Approbation — Archdiocese of Chicago
July 16, 2002

ISBN: 978-1-931709-42-2 (Inventory No. T25)
LCCN: 2002107483

Cover design by Monica Haneline
Cover photo depicts painting displayed in La Chiesa del Sacro Cuore del Suffragio, Rome; interior section illustration by Monica Haneline, based on a painting of St. Bernard's vision of souls being accompanied by angels from purgatory to heaven; the painting is displayed in La Chiesa della Santa Maria Scala Coeli, Rome

Interior design by Sherri L. Hoffman

PRINTED IN THE UNITED STATES OF AMERICA

To my mother and father,
Mary and Joseph Tassone,
who gave me the gift of life,
the gift of faith,
and my first holy Rosary.

Acknowledgments

This is the first Scriptural Rosary book for the souls in purgatory. In preparing this book I relied on a number of resources that played a key part in making this work what it is.

The following were invaluable references: *The Devotion of the Holy Rosary and the Five Scapulars*, by Michael Müller, C.SS.R., copyright © 1876 by Benzinger Brothers; *Meditations on the Rosary*, edited by Rev. Wilhelm Schaffler, translated by Silvia M. Welsh, copyright © 1929 by Verlag Ars Sacra and Joseph Mueller; *Our Lady's Rosary*, by Fathers Callan and McHugh of the Order of Preachers, copyright © 1939 by P. J. Kenedy and Sons; *Purgatory and the*

Means to Avoid It, by Rev. Martin Jugie, translated by Malachy Gerard Carroll, copyright © 1949 by The Newman Press; *St. Gertrude the Great*, copublished by Sands and Company and B. Herder Book Company, no date; *'Calls' from the Message of Fátima*, by Sister Lucia of Jesus and of the Immaculate Heart, translated by Sisters of Mosteiro de Santa Maria and Convento de N.S. do Bom Sucesso, Lisbon; distributed by The Ravengate Press, 2001.

The University of St. Mary of the Lake in Mundelein (Illinois) and Loyola University Chicago provided outstanding collections of works on purgatory.

I was moved by the works of Bishop Keppler, Very Rev. Dean Kinane, and Fathers Jugie, Lasance, Nageleisen, Sadlier, and Thurston, all of whom I call the "Purgatory Fathers." They guided me to the passages in Scripture, the understanding of purgatory, and the infinite mercy of God. To these authors I am most grateful.

I want to thank Jackie Lindsey, Our Sunday Visitor's Editorial Development Manager, who gave me the great privilege and honor of composing a Rosary for the holy souls and for the great Mother of God. As always, Steven Jay Gross provided his special unending support. Special thanks to Alida Antinori and Marcello Selmi, my tour guides in Italy, who led me to the church in Rome known as Sacro Cuore del Suffragio (as shown on the cover).

The Rosary is eternal. May God be praised and glorified, and Our Lady honored, forever.

Table of Contents

Foreword

Foreword

When I joined the Oblates of Mary Immaculate as a young man, Our Lady became, in a special way, part of my priesthood. Over the years, I am certain that it was Mary who guided me to a closer relationship with her Divine Son and the Church. There have been many occasions — too numerous to count — where Mary has interceded for me or for those whom I have entrusted to her care.

Sometimes one hears that Catholics do not know the Scriptures well enough. Yet, one of the ways in which we can best come to learn the Scriptures and meditate on them is through a Catholic method of prayer — the holy Rosary. The Rosary takes us on a "tour" of the Old and New Testaments, giving us the opportunity to call to mind the events that shaped the earthly life of Jesus and His mother, as well as those events that gave birth to the Church and changed the course of human history. These are the mysteries of the Catholic faith to which Holy Scripture gives written witness.

This little book will be an invaluable tool for those who have had a lifelong devotion to the Rosary, as well as for those who are learning the Rosary for the first time. The Scriptural meditations draw readers into a deeper experience of prayer, leading them beyond their intentions for personal needs to include petitions for the holy souls in purgatory, for the Church, and for the world.

It is my hope that all who use this book will be profoundly changed through the Rosary. May Our Lady intercede for you and for your families.

✠ FRANCIS CARDINAL GEORGE, O.M.I.
Archbishop of Chicago
July 16, 2002
Feast of Our Lady of Mount Carmel

Introduction

Introduction

O Virgin! Take this Rosary,
more precious far than gold;
'Tis woven with the life of Christ,
in holy gospels told.

(Lady Hungerforde's "Meditations upon the Beads," quoted by H. B. Feasey in *The Reliquary*, Vol. V, 1899)

The Rosary is one of the most beloved prayers of Catholics.

When we pray the most holy Rosary, we enter into the mysteries of the life, death, and resurrection of Our Lord and Savior, Jesus Christ. Saying the Rosary for the souls in purgatory is offering up to God all the merits, joys, sufferings, and death of our dear Savior for their relief.

The Holy Sacrifice of the Mass is the highest act of worship and highest form of prayer. Among private prayers and devotions, the Rosary is the greatest and most powerful form of mental and vocal prayer to assist the holy souls in purgatory to attain heaven.

During the Protestant Revolt in the sixteenth century and the French Revolution in the nineteenth century, when a priest was not available, a prayer service took the place of the Mass. The Offertory, Canon, and Holy Communion were omitted. Catholics were advised to say the Rosary and Mass prayers at home. As a result, the Rosary became known as the "Dry Mass."

Pope John Paul II tells us that the Rosary, like Scripture, echoes the rhythm of human life on earth and the afterlife. We pray the Scriptural Rosary for the "Church Suffering" to build up and join the "Church Triumphant." The beauty of praying a "Scriptural Rosary" for the suffering souls leads us to a richer knowledge of God's love and love of our neighbor.

This Scriptural Rosary gives us solid Biblical references to purgatory, as well as guidance on how to live and obtain the promise of eternal life. It also includes passages that show the penitent's concern, and emphasize mourning for their dead, as well as supplications to God, His justice, mercy, love, and reward.

Our Lady, the Queen of the Most Holy Rosary, is the mother of us all. She intercedes for the living and the dead. She also gives the holy souls great comfort and consolation. The Church recommends the Rosary as a prayer to save souls and to obtain peace in the world.

The Rosary is a most powerful prayer to obtain relief and release for the suffering souls in purgatory in that we not only offer up the prayers of the Rosary for them but also the indulgences attached to these prayers.

A *plenary indulgence* is granted when the Rosary is recited in a church or oratory or when it is recited by members of a family, a religious community, or a pious association.

A *partial indulgence* is granted for its recitation in all other circumstances.

The relief the souls receive from the Rosary depends on the fervor in which we say it. In a revelation when St. Gertrude asked Our Lord how many souls were delivered from purgatory by her prayers and those of her sisters, Our Lord replied, "The number is proportionate to the *zeal and fervor* of those who pray for them."[1]

The suffering souls in purgatory love, praise, and thank God. They are saved! But their greatest suffering is worse than any pain, illness, or loss on earth. They have seen the face of God! Now they know the goodness of God and want to be with Him but cannot. So the holy souls' loss of the sight of God is their greatest suffering. This is purgatory.

No sooner has the soul departed this life than it beholds God, and from this "sight" the soul receives at once so deep and vivid a knowledge of God and all His infinite perfections that it is utterly incapable of being occupied with anything other than the divine beauty and goodness. The soul feels so violently drawn toward God that it finds it altogether impossible to wish, to seek, and to love anything but God. The soul experiences at once an insatiable hunger and thirst after God; it pants for its supreme good with a most ardent desire. "God! God! I must be with God" is the soul's constant cry.

Souls undergo purification necessary for heaven . . . they never rest. They beg for our prayers and suffrages (that is, intercessions). We often hear, "Oh, the soul of this or that person is certainly in heaven." How often does this false charity cause souls to suffer and delay their entry into heaven? Let us rather be their advocate by our prayers and turn their pain into everlasting glory.

When we pray the Rosary for the holy souls, we gain fresh intercessors and also increase God's glory. "If we knew the power of their intercession," says St. John Vianney, "we would not be remiss in praying for them!"[2]

There are no ungrateful souls in heaven. Once souls enter heaven, they prostrate themselves before the throne of God and pray unceasingly for those who, through their prayers, helped release them from purgatory. They become our dearest and sincerest friends here on earth and in heaven for all eternity!

Remember to pray for the souls loved ones, for those consecrated t — priests and religious — for those abandoned, and for those closest to heaven. And the author would be indebted for one Hail Mary for her soul!

God has given us the awesome power and the privilege of assisting souls on their journey to Paradise. St. John Masias, known as the "Helper of the Poor Souls," offered three Rosaries every night for the souls in purgatory, praying for them on his knees despite bodily fatigue. The souls often appeared to him, begging his powerful intercession. "Give us prayers," they cried with one voice. "Oh, Brother John, you are the friend of the poor and sick! Be our friend, too! Help make us worthy to be with God and His blessed ones."[3]

St. John's friend, St. John the Evangelist, revealed to him that his prayers had released more than one million souls from their confinement. On his deathbed they escorted him into heaven.

Work while it is still day! Have mercy on yourselves. Pray the Rosary for the holy souls!

How to Recite the Rosary

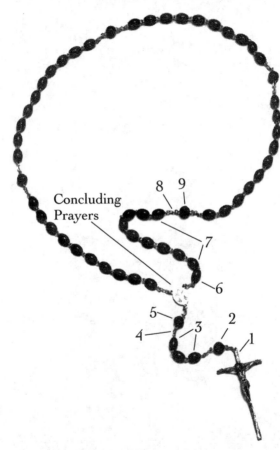

Concluding
Prayers

8 9
7
6
5
4 3
2
1

How to Recite the Rosary

❧

1. Make the Sign of the Cross, kiss the crucifix, and pray the Apostles' Creed.

2. Recite the Our Father on the large bead for Our Lady's intentions.

3. Pray three Hail Marys on the smaller beads for the gifts of faith, hope, and charity.

4. Pray the Glory Be.

Rosary Decades

5. Announce the First Mystery. Then, on the large bead, recite the Our Father.

6. Read the Scripture passage. Then pray the Hail Mary on the first small bead while meditating on the Mystery.

7. Continue this format for the remaining beads of the decade.

8. Conclude with the Glory Be, and then recite the Fátima Prayer.

9. Begin the next decade with the announcement of the Mystery, and then pray the Our Father. Repeat Steps 6, 7, and 8. Use this same format for the remaining Mysteries.

Concluding Prayers

- Recite the Hail, Holy Queen.

- Recite the Closing Prayer.

- Make the Sign of the Cross and kiss the crucifix.

Additional Rosary prayers are optional.

Five Tips for Praying a Fruitful Rosary

Five Tips for Praying a Fruitful Rosary

❧

The word "rosary" comes from the Latin *rosarium*, meaning "rose." We offer a beautiful rose for each Hail Mary to Our Lady. She presents this Rosary bouquet to her Son, Jesus.

1. *Love.* Center on the love Our Lord and His dear Mother have for each one of us and allow this love to penetrate your heart. If we knew how much they love us, we would cry for joy.

2. *Slowly.* Pray slowly "from the heart" so that you become one with the Mystery.

3. *Focus.* If you find your thoughts wandering, be gentle with yourself and allow

yourself to get back into the rhythm of the prayer.

4. *Suffering.* We all suffer. If you are ill or tired, offer your suffering to God in union with the crucified Christ on Calvary.

5. *Intentions.* Offer each decade for a particular intention, for example, the souls in purgatory, reparation for sins, a particular virtue, in thanksgiving.

Pope Pius XII tells us that "the soul, little by little, and imperceptibly, draws and assimilates the virtues the Mysteries contain."

Affectionate Salutations to Mary

Affectionate Salutations to Mary

I greet thee, Mary, Daughter of God the Father.

I greet thee, Mary, Mother of the Son of God.

I greet thee, Mary, Spouse of the Holy Spirit.

I greet thee, Mary, Temple of the Blessed Trinity.

I greet thee, Mary, white Lily of the resplendent Trinity.

I greet thee, Mary, fragrant Rose of the heavenly court.

I greet thee, Mary, Virgin full of meekness and humility, of whom the King of heaven willed to be born and nourished by thy milk.

I greet thee, Mary, Virgin of virgins.

I greet thee, Mary, Queen of Martyrs, whose soul was pierced by the sword of sorrows.

I greet thee, Mary, Queen of my heart, my sweetness, my life, and all my hope.

I greet thee, Mary, Mother most amiable.

I greet thee, Mary, Mother most admirable.

I greet thee, Mary, conceived without sin.

I greet thee, Mary, full of grace, the Lord is with thee, blessed art thou among women, and blessed be the fruit of thy womb.

Blessed be thy spouse, St. Joseph.

Blessed be thy father, St. Joachim.

Blessed be thy mother, St. Anne.

Blessed be thy angel, St. Gabriel.

Blessed be the Eternal Father, who hast chosen thee.

Blessed be thy Son, who hast loved thee.

Blessed be the Holy Spirit, who hast espoused thee.

May all those who love thee bless thee.

O Blessed Virgin, bless us and all in the name of thy dear Son. Amen.

(In a revelation to St. Gertrude, the Blessed Virgin made this promise: "To those who salute me thus, I will appear in such glory at the hour of death that they will anticipate the very joys of heaven."[4])

The Joyful Mysteries

The Joyful Mysteries

He was conceived by the power of the Holy Spirit and born of the Virgin Mary.

Alma Redemptoris Mater

Mother of Christ! hear thou thy
    people's cry,
Star of the deep, and portal of the sky.
Mother of Him Who thee from
    nothing made,
Sinking we strive and call to thee for
    aid.
Oh, by that joy which Gabriel brought
    to thee,
Pure Virgin, first and last, look on our
    misery.

FIRST JOYFUL MYSTERY

The Annunciation

Fruit of the Mystery: Humility

*To Him, O Virgin, whom you did conceive
by the power of the Holy Spirit!*

You are my refuge, O Lord!

✤ *Our Father*

"Strive for peace with all men, and for
the holiness without which no one will see
the Lord." — HEBREWS 12:14

✤ *Hail Mary*

"The LORD your God is a devouring
fire." — DEUTERONOMY 4:24

✤ *Hail Mary*

"No one in heaven or on earth or under the earth was able to open the scroll or to look into it." — REVELATION 5:3

🌹 *Hail Mary*

"Do not be afraid." — MATTHEW 28:10

🌹 *Hail Mary*

"Behold, I send an angel before you, to guard you on the way and to bring you to the place which I have prepared."
— EXODUS 23:20

🌹 *Hail Mary*

"God has not called us for uncleanness, but in holiness." — 1 THESSALONIANS 4:7

🌹 *Hail Mary*

"The LORD our God is holy!"

— PSALM 99:9

✠ *Hail Mary*

"O the depth of the riches and wisdom and knowledge of God! How unsearchable are his judgments and how inscrutable his ways!" — ROMANS 11:33

✠ *Hail Mary*

"And above all these put on love, which binds everything together in perfect harmony." — COLOSSIANS 3:14

✠ *Hail Mary*

"With God nothing will be impossible."

— LUKE 1:37

✠ *Hail Mary*

❧ *Glory Be*

O my Jesus, forgive us our sins. Save us from the fires of hell. Lead all souls to heaven, especially those who are in most need of your mercy. And console the souls in purgatory, particularly those most abandoned.

SECOND JOYFUL MYSTERY

The Visitation

Fruit of the Mystery: Charity

*To Him, O Virgin, whom you did
carry to Elizabeth!*

Deliver them, O Lord!

❧ *Our Father*

"Have pity on me, have pity on me, / O
you my friends, / for the hand of God has
touched me!" — JOB 19:21

❧ *Hail Mary*

"Wash me thoroughly from my iniquity,
/ and cleanse me from my sin!"

— PSALM 51:2

❧ *Hail Mary*

"Do good to a godly man and you will be repaid — / if not by him, certainly by the Most High." — SIRACH 12:2

🌹 *Hail Mary*

"Blessed are the merciful, for they shall obtain mercy." — MATTHEW 5:7

🌹 *Hail Mary*

"Unless you repent you will all likewise perish." — LUKE 13:5

🌹 *Hail Mary*

"Every one will be salted with fire."
                                    — MARK 9:49

🌹 *Hail Mary*

"Nothing unclean shall enter it."

— REVELATION 21:27

✹ *Hail Mary*

"If the righteous man is scarcely saved, / where will the impious and sinner appear?"

— 1 PETER 4:18

✹ *Hail Mary*

"If we hope for what we do not see, we wait for it with patience." — ROMANS 8:25

✹ *Hail Mary*

"So you have sorrow now, but I will see you again and your hearts will rejoice, and no one will take your joy from you."

— JOHN 16:22

✹ *Hail Mary*

🌹 Glory Be

O my Jesus, forgive us our sins. Save
us from the fires of hell. Lead all souls to
heaven, especially those who are in most
need of your mercy. And console the souls
in purgatory, particularly those most abandoned.

THIRD JOYFUL MYSTERY

The Nativity

Fruit of the Mystery:
Detachment from the world

To Him, O Virgin, to whom you gave birth!

Give them joy, O Lord!

✠ *Our Father*

"We know that the whole creation has been groaning in travail together until now."
— ROMANS 8:22

✠ *Hail Mary*

"You also must be ready; for the Son of man is coming at an hour you do not expect." — LUKE 12:40

✠ *Hail Mary*

"Who can endure the day of his coming, and who can stand when he appears?"
— MALACHI 3:2

✣ Hail Mary

"Lift up your heads, O gates! / and be lifted up, O ancient doors! / that the King of glory may come in." — PSALM 24:7

✣ Hail Mary

"As his majesty is, / so also is his mercy."
— SIRACH 2:18

✣ Hail Mary

"He will swallow up death forever."
— ISAIAH 25:8

✣ Hail Mary

"Truly, I say to you, unless you turn and become like children, you will never enter the kingdom of heaven." — MATTHEW 18:3

✌ *Hail Mary*

"May the Lord make you increase and abound in love . . . so that he may establish your hearts unblamable in holiness before our God and Father, at the coming of our Lord Jesus with all his saints."

— 1 THESSALONIANS 3:12-13

✌ *Hail Mary*

"Since we have these promises, beloved, let us cleanse ourselves from every defilement of body and spirit, and make holiness perfect in the fear of God."

— 2 CORINTHIANS 7:1

✌ *Hail Mary*

"And I heard every creature in heaven and on earth and under the earth and in the sea, and all therein, saying, 'To him who sits upon the throne and to the Lamb be blessing and honor and glory and might for ever and ever!' " — REVELATION 5:13

❧ *Hail Mary*

❧ *Glory Be*

O my Jesus, forgive us our sins. Save us from the fires of hell. Lead all souls to heaven, especially those who are in most need of your mercy. And console the souls in purgatory, particularly those most abandoned.

FOURTH JOYFUL MYSTERY

The Presentation

Fruit of the Mystery: Purity

To Him, O Virgin, whom you did offer up in the Temple!

Spare them, O Lord!

Our Father

"We have beheld his glory."

— JOHN 1:14

Hail Mary

"He will sit as a refiner and purifier of silver, and he will purify the sons of Levi and refine them like gold and silver, till they present right offerings to the LORD."

— MALACHI 3:3

Hail Mary

"You may have to suffer various trials, that the genuineness of your faith, more precious than gold which though perishable is tested by fire, may redound to praise and glory and honor at the revelation of Jesus Christ." — 1 PETER 1:6-7

❧ *Hail Mary*

"The souls of the righteous are in the hand of God, / and no torment will ever touch them." — WISDOM 3:1

❧ *Hail Mary*

"Many shall purify themselves, and make themselves white, and be refined."
                                    — DANIEL 12:10

❧ *Hail Mary*

"What do people mean by being baptized on behalf of the dead? If the dead are not raised at all, why are people baptized on their behalf?" — 1 CORINTHIANS 15:29

🌹 *Hail Mary*

"Thou didst let men ride over our heads; / we went through fire and through water; / yet thou hast brought us forth to a spacious place." — PSALM 66:12

🌹 *Hail Mary*

"The fear of the Lord is wisdom and instruction." — SIRACH 1:27

🌹 *Hail Mary*

"If you have many possessions, make your gift from them in proportion." — TOBIT 4:8

🌹 *Hail Mary*

"He who closes his ear to the cry of the poor / will himself cry out and not be heard."
— PROVERBS 21:13

❧ *Hail Mary*

❧ *Glory Be*

O my Jesus, forgive us our sins. Save us from the fires of hell. Lead all souls to heaven, especially those who are in most need of your mercy. And console the souls in purgatory, particularly those most abandoned.

FIFTH JOYFUL MYSTERY

The Finding of the Child Jesus in the Temple

Fruit of the Mystery:
Obedience to the will of God

To Him, O Virgin, whom you did
find in the Temple!

Hear them, O Lord!

✠ *Our Father*

"The Judge is standing at the doors."
— JAMES 5:9

✠ *Hail Mary*

"We must work the works of him who sent me, while it is day; night comes, when no one can work." — JOHN 9:4

✠ *Hail Mary*

"Behold, the LORD will come in fire, / . . . by fire will the LORD execute judgment." — ISAIAH 66:15, 16

❧ *Hail Mary*

"I tell you, make friends for yourselves by means of unrighteous mammon, so that when it fails they may receive you into the eternal habitations." — LUKE 16:9

❧ *Hail Mary*

"I do not mean that others should be eased and you burdened, but that as a matter of equality your abundance at the present time should supply their want, so that their abundance may supply your want, that there may be equality."
— 2 CORINTHIANS 8:13-14

❧ *Hail Mary*

"Remember those who are in prison, as though in prison with them."

— HEBREWS 13:3

❧ *Hail Mary*

"Having been disciplined a little, they will receive great good, / because God tested them and found them worthy of himself."

— WISDOM 3:5

❧ *Hail Mary*

"My soul thirsts for God, / for the living God." — PSALM 42:2

❧ *Hail Mary*

"Water extinguishes a blazing fire: / so almsgiving atones for sin." — SIRACH 3:30

❧ *Hail Mary*

"You, therefore, must be perfect, as your heavenly Father is perfect."

— MATTHEW 5:48

❧ *Hail Mary*

❧ *Glory Be*

O my Jesus, forgive us our sins. Save us from the fires of hell. Lead all souls to heaven, especially those who are in most need of your mercy. And console the souls in purgatory, particularly those most abandoned.

The Luminous Mysteries

The Luminous Mysteries

I believe in Jesus Christ, his only Son, our Lord.

Salve Regina

Hail, holy Queen, Mother of Mercy!
Hail, our life, our sweetness, and our hope!
To thee do we cry, poor banished children
    of Eve.
To thee do we send up our sighs,
    mourning, and weeping in this vale of
    tears.
Turn then, most gracious advocate, thine
    eyes of mercy toward us.
And after this our exile, show unto us the
    blessed fruit of thy womb, Jesus.
O clement, O loving, O sweet Virgin
    Mary.

FIRST LUMINOUS MYSTERY

The Baptism of Our Lord

Fruit of the Mystery:
Openness to the Holy Spirit

He who was baptized by John in the Jordan!

Fill them with your spirit, O Lord!

❧ *Our Father*

"Blessed are those who wash their robes, that they may have the right to the tree of life." — REVELATION 22:14

❧ *Hail Mary*

"Repent, and be baptized every one of you in the name of Jesus Christ for the forgiveness of your sins; and you shall receive the gift of the Holy Spirit." — ACTS 2:38

❧ *Hail Mary*

"He humbled himself and became obedient unto death." — PHILIPPIANS 2:8

✠ *Hail Mary*

"So shall my word be that goes forth from my mouth; / it shall not return to me empty." — ISAIAH 55:11

✠ *Hail Mary*

"Do you not know that God's kindness is meant to lead you to repentance?"
— ROMANS 2:4

✠ *Hail Mary*

"All the ways of a man are pure in his own eyes, / but the LORD weighs the spirit."
— PROVERBS 16:2

✠ *Hail Mary*

"Purify your conscience from dead works to serve the living God."
                                    — HEBREWS 9:14

❧ *Hail Mary*

"Blessed are the pure in heart, for they shall see God." — MATTHEW 5:8

❧ *Hail Mary*

"For God so loved the world that he gave his only Son." — JOHN 3:16

❧ *Hail Mary*

"Precious in the sight of the LORD is the death of his saints." — PSALM 116:15

❧ *Hail Mary*

Glory Be

O my Jesus, forgive us our sins. Save us from the fires of hell. Lead all souls to heaven, especially those who are in most need of your mercy. And console the souls in purgatory, particularly those most abandoned.

SECOND LUMINOUS MYSTERY

The Wedding Feast at Cana

Fruit of the Mystery: Fidelity

He who turned water into wine!

Fill them with your love, O Lord!

❧ *Our Father*

"His mother said to the servants, 'Do whatever he tells you.' " — JOHN 2:5

❧ *Hail Mary*

"Ask, and it will be given you; seek, and you will find; knock, and it will be opened to you." — MATTHEW 7:7

❧ *Hail Mary*

"No one who believes in him will be put to shame." — ROMANS 10:11

🌹 *Hail Mary*

"For thou art God of the lowly, helper of the oppressed, upholder of the weak, protector of the forlorn, savior of those without hope." — JUDITH 9:11

🌹 *Hail Mary*

"Truly I perceive that God shows no partiality, but in every nation any one who fears him and does what is right is acceptable to him." — ACTS 10:34-35

🌹 *Hail Mary*

"Whoever honors his father atones for sins, / and whoever glorifies his mother is like one who lays up treasure."

— SIRACH 3:3-4

🌹 *Hail Mary*

"He saved us, not because of deeds done by us in righteousness, but in virtue of his own mercy." — TITUS 3:5

🌹 *Hail Mary*

"Let him who boasts, boast of the Lord."

— 1 CORINTHIANS 1:31

🌹 *Hail Mary*

"O LORD my God, I will give thanks to thee for ever." — PSALM 30:12

🌹 *Hail Mary*

"Humble yourselves therefore under the mighty hand of God, that in due time he may exalt you." — 1 PETER 5:6

🌹 *Hail Mary*

🌹 *Glory Be*

O my Jesus, forgive us our sins. Save us from the fires of hell. Lead all souls to heaven, especially those who are in most need of your mercy. And console the souls in purgatory, particularly those most abandoned.

THIRD LUMINOUS MYSTERY

The Proclamation of the Kingdom

Fruit of the Mystery:
Repentance and trust in God

He who went about preaching the reign of God!

Fill them with your peace, O Lord!

✠ *Our Father*

"Go into all the world and preach the gospel to the whole creation."

— MARK 16:15

✠ *Hail Mary*

"Truly, truly, I say to you, unless a grain of wheat falls into the earth and dies, it remains alone; but if it dies, it bears much fruit." — JOHN 12:24

✠ *Hail Mary*

"The fruit of the Spirit is love, joy, peace, patience, kindness, goodness, faithfulness, gentleness, self-control."

— GALATIANS 5:22-23

✜ *Hail Mary*

"I have come to do thy will, O God."

— HEBREWS 10:7

✜ *Hail Mary*

"One thing have I asked of the LORD, that will I seek after; / that I may dwell in the house of the LORD / all the days of my life." — PSALM 27:4

✜ *Hail Mary*

"Do the work of an evangelist, fulfill your ministry." — 2 TIMOTHY 4:5

✜ *Hail Mary*

"Do you not know that you are God's temple and that God's Spirit dwells in you?" — 1 CORINTHIANS 3:16

🌹 *Hail Mary*

"He is not God of the dead, but of the living." — MATTHEW 22:32

🌹 *Hail Mary*

"But you are a chosen race, a royal priesthood, a holy nation, God's own people." — 1 PETER 2:9

🌹 *Hail Mary*

"Come, let us walk in the light of the LORD." — ISAIAH 2:5

🌹 *Hail Mary*

❧ Glory Be

O my Jesus, forgive us our sins. Save us from the fires of hell. Lead all souls to heaven, especially those who are in most need of your mercy. And console the souls in purgatory, particularly those most abandoned.

FOURTH LUMINOUS MYSTERY

The Transfiguration

Fruit of the Mystery: Desire for holiness

He who was transfigured on the Mount!

Fill them with your glory, O Lord!

🌹 *Our Father*

"He was transfigured before them, and his garments became glistening, intensely white, as no fuller on earth could bleach them." — MARK 9:2-3

🌹 *Hail Mary*

"A voice came out of the cloud, saying, 'This is my Son, my Chosen; listen to him!'"
— LUKE 9:35

🌹 *Hail Mary*

"We all, with unveiled face, beholding the glory of the Lord, are being changed into his likeness from one degree of glory to another." — 2 CORINTHIANS 3:18

🌹 *Hail Mary*

"And so observe, from generation to generation, that none who put their trust in him will lack strength."

— 1 MACCABEES 2:61

🌹 *Hail Mary*

"You are the light of the world. Let your light so shine before men, that they may see your good works and give glory to your Father who is in heaven."

— MATTHEW 5:14, 16

🌹 *Hail Mary*

"The peace of God, which passes all understanding, will keep your hearts and your minds in Christ Jesus."

— PHILIPPIANS 4:7

✠ Hail Mary

"The LORD is my chosen portion and my cup; / thou holdest my lot." — PSALM 16:5

✠ Hail Mary

"Now that you have been set free from sin and have become slaves of God, the return you get is sanctification and its end, eternal life." — ROMANS 6:22

✠ Hail Mary

"Those who are wise shall shine like the brightness of the firmament; and those who turn many to righteousness, like the stars for ever and ever." — DANIEL 12:3

✤ *Hail Mary*

"Night shall be no more; they need no light of lamp or sun, for the Lord God will be their light, and they shall reign for ever and ever." — REVELATION 22:5

✤ *Hail Mary*

✤ *Glory Be*

O my Jesus, forgive us our sins. Save us from the fires of hell. Lead all souls to heaven, especially those who are in most need of your mercy. And console the souls in purgatory, particularly those most abandoned.

FIFTH LUMINOUS MYSTERY

The Institution of the Eucharist

Fruit of the Mystery: Adoration

He who gave us His Body and Blood!

Fill them with the bread of life, O Lord!

❧ *Our Father*

"I am the living bread which came down from heaven; if any one eats of this bread, he will live for ever." — JOHN 6:51

❧ *Hail Mary*

"This is my blood of the covenant, which is poured out for many." — MARK 14:24

❧ *Hail Mary*

"I am not aware of anything against myself, but I am not thereby acquitted. It is the Lord who judges me."

— 1 Corinthians 4:4

❧ Hail Mary

"I will lift up the cup of salvation and call on the name of the Lord."

— Psalm 116:13

❧ Hail Mary

"I am sure that he who began a good work in you will bring it to completion at the day of Jesus Christ."

— Philippians 1:6

❧ Hail Mary

"Thy dead shall live, their bodies shall rise. / O dwellers in the dust, awake and sing for joy!" — ISAIAH 26:19

🌹 *Hail Mary*

"Whether we live or whether we die, we are the Lord's." — ROMANS 14:8

🌹 *Hail Mary*

"Be zealous to be found by him without spot or blemish, and at peace."
— 2 PETER 3:14

🌹 *Hail Mary*

"I am with you always, to the close of the age." — MATTHEW 28:20

🌹 *Hail Mary*

" 'Surely I am coming soon.' Amen. Come, Lord Jesus!" — REVELATION 22:20

❧ *Hail Mary*

❧ *Glory Be*

O my Jesus, forgive us our sins. Save us from the fires of hell. Lead all souls to heaven, especially those who are in most need of your mercy. And console the souls in purgatory, particularly those most abandoned.

The Sorrowful Mysteries

The Sorrowful Mysteries

He suffered under Pontius Pilate, was crucified, died, and was buried.

Ave Regina Caelorum
Hail, O Queen of heaven enthroned!
Hail, by angels Mistress owned!
Root of Jesse! Gate of morn,
Whence the world's true Light
    was born.
Glorious Virgin, joy to thee,
Beautiful surpassingly!
Fairest thou where all art fair!
Plead with Christ our sins to spare.
Make me worthy to praise thee,
    O Blessed Virgin.
Give me strength against thine
    enemies.

FIRST SORROWFUL MYSTERY

The Agony in the Garden

Fruit of the Mystery: Fervor in prayer

He who sweat blood for us!

Thy will be done, O Lord!

🌹 *Our Father*

"In the days of his flesh, Jesus offered up prayers and supplications, with loud cries and tears." — HEBREWS 5:7

🌹 *Hail Mary*

"The cords of Sheol entangled me, / the snares of death confronted me."

— 2 SAMUEL 22:6

🌹 *Hail Mary*

"The sacrifice acceptable to God is a broken spirit; / a broken and contrite heart, O God, thou wilt not despise." — PSALM 51:17

✤ *Hail Mary*

"Prayer is good when accompanied by fasting, almsgiving, and righteousness."
— TOBIT 12:8

✤ *Hail Mary*

"Truly, I say to you, you will never get out till you have paid the last penny."
— MATTHEW 5:26

✤ *Hail Mary*

"He called out, 'Father Abraham, have mercy upon me, and send Lazarus to dip the end of his finger in water and cool my tongue; for I am in anguish in this flame.' "

— LUKE 16:24

Hail Mary

"As for you also, because of the blood of my covenant with you, / I will set your captives free from the waterless pit."

— ZECHARIAH 9:11

Hail Mary

"You yourselves know well that the day of the Lord will come like a thief in the night." — 1 THESSALONIANS 5:2

Hail Mary

"He will bring me forth to the light; / I shall behold his deliverance." — MICAH 7:9

Hail Mary

"Stretch forth your hand to the poor, /
so that your blessing may be complete."

— SIRACH 7:32

✹ *Hail Mary*

✹ *Glory Be*

O my Jesus, forgive us our sins. Save
us from the fires of hell. Lead all souls to
heaven, especially those who are in most
need of your mercy. And console the souls
in purgatory, particularly those most abandoned.

SECOND SORROWFUL MYSTERY

The Scourging at the Pillar

Fruit of the Mystery: Mortification

He was scourged for our sake!

Cleanse them, O Lord!

Our Father

"These things you have done and I have been silent; / you thought that I was one like yourself. / But now I rebuke you, and lay the charge before you." — PSALM 50:21

Hail Mary

"That servant who knew his master's will, but did not make ready or act according to his will, shall receive a severe beating." — LUKE 12:47

🌹 *Hail Mary*

"He bore the sin of many, / and made intercession for the transgressors."

— ISAIAH 53:12

🌹 *Hail Mary*

"Do not fear what you are about to suffer." — REVELATION 2:10

🌹 *Hail Mary*

"When we are judged by the Lord, we are chastened so that we may not be condemned along with the world."

— 1 CORINTHIANS 11:32

🌹 *Hail Mary*

"The Lord disciplines him whom he loves, / and chastises every son whom he receives." — HEBREWS 12:6

❧ *Hail Mary*

"Unless one is born anew, he cannot see the kingdom of God." — JOHN 3:3

❧ *Hail Mary*

"Enter by the narrow gate."
— MATTHEW 7:13

❧ *Hail Mary*

"Let us not grow weary in well-doing, for in due season we shall reap, if we do not lose heart." — GALATIANS 6:9

❧ *Hail Mary*

"May the Lord grant him to find mercy from the Lord on that Day."

— 2 TIMOTHY 1:18

❧ *Hail Mary*

❧ *Glory Be*

O my Jesus, forgive us our sins. Save us from the fires of hell. Lead all souls to heaven, especially those who are in most need of your mercy. And console the souls in purgatory, particularly those most abandoned.

THIRD SORROWFUL MYSTERY

The Crowning with Thorns

Fruit of the Mystery: Courage

He who for our sake was crowned with thorns!

Show them Your face, O Lord!

✸ *Our Father*

"Thou hast said, 'Seek ye my face.' / My heart says to thee, / 'Thy face, LORD, do I seek.' / Hide not thy face from me."
— PSALM 27:8-9

✸ *Hail Mary*

"The crucible is for silver, and the furnace is for gold, / and the LORD tries hearts."
— PROVERBS 17:3

✸ *Hail Mary*

"Pray for one another, that you may be healed." — JAMES 5:16

🌹 *Hail Mary*

"Save some, by snatching them out of the fire." — JUDE 23

🌹 *Hail Mary*

"Give graciously to all the living, / and withhold not kindness from the dead."

— SIRACH 7:33

🌹 *Hail Mary*

"The King will answer them, 'Truly, I say to you, as you did it to one of the least of these my brethren, you did it to me.'"

— MATTHEW 25:40

🌹 *Hail Mary*

"Judge not, and you will not be judged. . . . For the measure you give will be the measure you get back." — LUKE 6:37-38

🌹 Hail Mary

"Whenever you stand praying, forgive, if you have anything against anyone."
— MARK 11:25

🌹 Hail Mary

"Bear one another's burdens."
— GALATIANS 6:2

🌹 Hail Mary

"God will bring every deed into judgment, with every secret thing, whether good or evil." — ECCLESIASTES 12:14

🌹 Hail Mary

🌹 Glory Be

O my Jesus, forgive us our sins. Save us from the fires of hell. Lead all souls to heaven, especially those who are in most need of your mercy. And console the souls in purgatory, particularly those most abandoned.

FOURTH SORROWFUL MYSTERY

The Carrying of the Cross

Fruit of the Mystery: Perseverance

He who bore the heavy Cross for our sins!

Intercede for them, O Lord!

❧ *Our Father*

"Sir, I have no man to put me into the pool." — JOHN 5:6

❧ *Hail Mary*

"Break off your sins by practicing righteousness, and your iniquities by showing mercy to the oppressed." — DANIEL 4:27

❧ *Hail Mary*

"Bear fruits that befit repentance."

— Luke 3:8

🌹 *Hail Mary*

"Beloved, do not be surprised at the fiery ordeal which comes upon you to prove you, as though something strange were happening to you." — 1 Peter 4:12

🌹 *Hail Mary*

"Count it all joy, my brethren, when you meet various trials, for you know that the testing of your faith produces steadfastness." — James 1:2

🌹 *Hail Mary*

"This is evidence of the righteous judgment of God, that you may be made worthy of the kingdom of God, for which you are suffering." — 2 THESSALONIANS 1:5

🌹 *Hail Mary*

"Even though I walk through the valley of the shadow of death, / I fear no evil; / for thou art with me; / thy rod and thy staff, / they comfort me." — PSALM 23:4

🌹 *Hail Mary*

"In all you do, remember the end of your life, / and then you will never sin."
                                        — SIRACH 7:36

🌹 *Hail Mary*

"You shall love the LORD your God with all your heart, and with all your soul, and with all your might." — DEUTERONOMY 6:5

🌹 *Hail Mary*

"Where your treasure is, there will your heart be also." — MATTHEW 6:21

🌹 *Hail Mary*

🌹 *Glory Be*

O my Jesus, forgive us our sins. Save us from the fires of hell. Lead all souls to heaven, especially those who are in most need of your mercy. And console the souls in purgatory, particularly those most abandoned.

FIFTH SORROWFUL MYSTERY

The Crucifixion

Fruit of the Mystery: Forgiveness

He who died for us!

Have mercy on our dead, O Lord!

🌹 *Our Father*

"Jesus, Son of David, have mercy on me!" — MARK 10:47

🌹 *Hail Mary*

"Out of the depths I cry to thee, O LORD! / Lord, hear my voice!"
— PSALM 130:1

🌹 *Hail Mary*

"The sinners in Zion are afraid; / trembling has seized the godless: / 'Who among us can dwell with the devouring fire?' "

— ISAIAH 33:14

Hail Mary

"If any man's work is burned up, he will suffer loss, though he himself will be saved, but only as through fire."

— 1 CORINTHIANS 3:15

Hail Mary

"Like gold in the furnace he tried them, and like a sacrificial burnt offering he accepted them." — WISDOM 3:6

Hail Mary

"The people of Israel wept for Moses in the plains of Moab thirty days."
— Deuteronomy 34:8

✠ *Hail Mary*

"You are dust, / and to dust you shall return." — Genesis 3:19

✠ *Hail Mary*

"Blessed are those who mourn, for they shall be comforted." — Matthew 5:4

✠ *Hail Mary*

"Therefore he made atonement for the dead, that they might be delivered from their sin." — 2 Maccabees 12:45

✠ *Hail Mary*

"Jesus, remember me when you come in your kingly power." — LUKE 23:42

✿ *Hail Mary*

✿ *Glory Be*

O my Jesus, forgive us our sins. Save us from the fires of hell. Lead all souls to heaven, especially those who are in most need of your mercy. And console the souls in purgatory, particularly those most abandoned.

The Glorious Mysteries

The Glorious Mysteries

He descended to the dead. On the third day he rose again. He ascended into heaven, and is seated at the right hand of the Father. He will come again to judge the living and the dead.

Regina Coeli
Joy to thee, O Queen of heaven!
   Alleluia!
He whom it was thine to bear.
   Alleluia!
As He promised, has risen. Alleluia!
Plead for us a pitying prayer. Alleluia!
Rejoice and be glad, O Virgin Mary!
   Alleluia!
Because the Lord is truly risen.
   Alleluia!

FIRST GLORIOUS MYSTERY

The Resurrection

Fruit of the Mystery: Faith

He who rose from the dead!

Raise them up, O Lord!

❧ *Our Father*

"Bring me out of prison, / that I may give thanks to thy name!" — PSALM 142:7

❧ *Hail Mary*

"O death, where is thy victory? / O death, where is thy sting?"
            — 1 CORINTHIANS 15:55

❧ *Hail Mary*

"We would not have you ignorant, brethren, concerning those who are asleep, that you may not grieve as others do who have no hope." — 1 THESSALONIANS 4:13

🌹 *Hail Mary*

"I died, and behold I am alive for evermore." — REVELATION 1:17

🌹 *Hail Mary*

"I am the resurrection and the life."
— JOHN 11:25

🌹 *Hail Mary*

"At the name of Jesus every knee should bow, in heaven and on earth and under the earth." — PHILIPPIANS 2:10

🌹 *Hail Mary*

"He went and preached to the spirits in prison, who formerly did not obey."

— 1 PETER 3:19

✥ *Hail Mary*

"Awake, O sleeper, and arise from the dead, / and Christ shall give you light."

— EPHESIANS 5:14

✥ *Hail Mary*

"I will remember their sins no more."

— HEBREWS 8:12

✥ *Hail Mary*

"I know that my Redeemer lives, / and at last he will stand upon the earth."

— JOB 19:25

✥ *Hail Mary*

🌹 Glory Be

O my Jesus, forgive us our sins. Save us from the fires of hell. Lead all souls to heaven, especially those who are in most need of your mercy. And console the souls in purgatory, particularly those most abandoned.

SECOND GLORIOUS MYSTERY

The Ascension

Fruit of the Mystery: Hope

He who did ascend into heaven!

Come, Lord Jesus, for these souls!

🌹 *Our Father*

"When he ascended on high he led a host of captives, / and he gave gifts to men." — EPHESIANS 4:8

🌹 *Hail Mary*

"This is why the gospel was preached even to the dead, that though judged in the flesh like men, they might live in the spirit like God." — 1 PETER 4:6

🌹 *Hail Mary*

"Truly, I say to you, whatever you bind on earth shall be bound in heaven, and whatever you loose on earth shall be loosed in heaven." — MATTHEW 18:18

🌹 *Hail Mary*

"Great is thy steadfast love toward me; / thou hast delivered my soul from the depths of Sheol." — PSALM 86:13

🌹 *Hail Mary*

"Grace and mercy are upon his elect."
— WISDOM 3:9

🌹 *Hail Mary*

"He cried with a loud voice, 'Lazarus, come out.' " — JOHN 11:43

🌹 *Hail Mary*

"The trumpet will sound, and the dead will be raised imperishable, and we shall be changed." — 1 CORINTHIANS 15:52

❧ *Hail Mary*

"If we have died with him, we shall also live with him." — 2 TIMOTHY 2:11

❧ *Hail Mary*

"To him who loves us and has freed us from our sins by his blood . . . to him be glory and dominion for ever and ever."
— REVELATION 1:5-6

❧ *Hail Mary*

"But remember me, when it is well with you, and do me the kindness, I pray you, to make mention of me." — GENESIS 40:14

❧ *Hail Mary*

🌹 Glory Be

O my Jesus, forgive us our sins. Save us from the fires of hell. Lead all souls to heaven, especially those who are in most need of your mercy. And console the souls in purgatory, particularly those most abandoned.

THIRD GLORIOUS MYSTERY

Descent of the Holy Spirit

Fruit of the Mystery: Gifts of the Holy Spirit

He who sent down the Holy Spirit!

Console them, O Lord!

✹ *Our Father*

"Whoever says a word against the Son of man will be forgiven; but whoever speaks against the Holy Spirit will not be forgiven, either in this age or in the age to come."

— MATTHEW 12:32

✹ *Hail Mary*

"The Lord shall have washed away the filth of the daughters of Zion and cleansed the bloodstains of Jerusalem from its midst by a spirit of judgment and by a spirit of burning." — ISAIAH 4:4

🌹 *Hail Mary*

"Love is as strong as death, . . . / Its flashes are flashes of fire."

— SONG OF SOLOMON 8:6

🌹 *Hail Mary*

"The prayer of a righteous man has great power in its effects." — JAMES 5:16

🌹 *Hail Mary*

"I brought a reminder of your prayer before the Holy One; and when you buried the dead, I was likewise present with you."

— TOBIT 12:12

🌹 *Hail Mary*

"A man who is kind benefits himself."
— Proverbs 11:17

🌹 *Hail Mary*

"Let not your hearts be troubled; believe in God, believe also in me. In my Father's house are many rooms." — John 14:1

🌹 *Hail Mary*

"Our feet have been standing / within your gates, O Jerusalem!" — Psalm 122:2

🌹 *Hail Mary*

"For to me to live is Christ, and to die is gain." — Philippians 1:21

🌹 *Hail Mary*

"He is the beginning, the firstborn from the dead." — Colossians 1:18

❧ *Hail Mary*

❧ *Glory Be*

O my Jesus, forgive us our sins. Save us from the fires of hell. Lead all souls to heaven, especially those who are in most need of your mercy. And console the souls in purgatory, particularly those most abandoned.

FOURTH GLORIOUS MYSTERY

The Assumption

Fruit of the Mystery: Union with Christ

He, O Virgin, who received you into heaven!

You are my hope, O Lord!

✤ *Our Father*

"He drew me up from the desolate pit."
— PSALM 40:2

✤ *Hail Mary*

"Rejoice in the Lord always; again I will say, Rejoice. Let all men know your forbearance." — PHILIPPIANS 4:4-5

✤ *Hail Mary*

"Judgment is without mercy to one who has shown no mercy; yet mercy triumphs over judgment." — JAMES 2:13

🌹 Hail Mary

"The hour is coming, and now is, when the dead will hear the voice of the Son of God, and those who hear will live."

— JOHN 5:25

🌹 Hail Mary

"The Lord GOD will wipe away tears from all faces." — ISAIAH 25:8

🌹 Hail Mary

"We know that if the earthly tent we live in is destroyed, we have a building from God, a house not made with hands, eternal in the heavens." — 2 CORINTHIANS 5:1

🌹 Hail Mary

"We know that in everything God works for good with those who love him."
— ROMANS 8:28

🌹 *Hail Mary*

"Trust in the LORD with all your heart."
— PROVERBS 3:5

🌹 *Hail Mary*

"I heard a voice from heaven saying, 'Write this: Blessed are the dead who die in the Lord henceforth.' 'Blessed indeed,' says the Spirit, 'that they may rest from their labors, for their deeds follow them!' "
— REVELATION 14:13

🌹 *Hail Mary*

"Praise God and give thanks to him; exalt him and give thanks to him in the presence of all the living for what he has done for you." — Tobit 12:6

❧ *Hail Mary*

❧ *Glory Be*

O my Jesus, forgive us our sins. Save us from the fires of hell. Lead all souls to heaven, especially those who are in most need of your mercy. And console the souls in purgatory, particularly those most abandoned.

FIFTH GLORIOUS MYSTERY

The Coronation

Fruit of the Mystery: Confidence in Mary

He, O Virgin, who crowned you in heaven!

Lord, in Your steadfast love, give them eternal rest!

🌹 *Our Father*

"Today you will be with me in Paradise."
— LUKE 23:43

🌹 *Hail Mary*

"Who shall separate us from the love of Christ?" — ROMANS 8:35

🌹 *Hail Mary*

"I have swept away your transgressions like a cloud, / and your sins like mist; / return to me, for I have redeemed you."

— ISAIAH 44:22

✠ Hail Mary

" 'What no eye has seen, nor ear heard, nor heart of man conceived, / what God has prepared for those who love him,' God has revealed to us through the Spirit."

— 1 CORINTHIANS 2:9-10

✠ Hail Mary

"The LORD has chastened me sorely, / but he has not given me over to death."

— PSALM 118:18

✠ Hail Mary

"By his wounds you have been healed."
— 1 PETER 2:24

❧ *Hail Mary*

"To him be the glory for ever and ever."
— 2 TIMOTHY 4:18

❧ *Hail Mary*

"May the LORD deal kindly with you, as you have dealt with the dead." — RUTH 1:8

❧ *Hail Mary*

"Be faithful unto death, and I will give you the crown of life." — REVELATION 2:10

❧ *Hail Mary*

"Come, O blessed of my Father, inherit the kingdom prepared for you from the foundation of the world." — MATTHEW 25:34

❧ *Hail Mary*

✿ Glory Be

O my Jesus, forgive us our sins. Save us from the fires of hell. Lead all souls to heaven, especially those who are in most need of your mercy. And console the souls in purgatory, particularly those most abandoned.

Litany of Our Lady of Montligeon on Behalf of the Holy Souls

Litany of Our Lady of Montligeon on Behalf of the Holy Souls

❧

Lord, have mercy on our dead,
*especially those in dire need of
your mercy.*
Christ, have mercy on our dead,
*especially those in dire need of
your mercy.*
Lord, have mercy on our dead,
*especially those in dire need of
your mercy.*
Christ, hear us. *Christ, graciously
hear us.*

Mary, daughter of the Eternal Father,
pray for our dead.

Mary, mother of the redeemer of mankind, *pray for our dead.*

Mary, temple of the Holy Spirit . . .

Mary, chosen by God from all eternity . . .

Mary, dawn of the Sun of Justice . . .

Mary, conceived without original sin . . .

Mary, on whom the devil had no power . . .

Mary, whose body never passed through the corruption of the tomb . . .

Mary, whom Jesus wrapped into his glory . . .

Mary, whose throne is near Jesus . . .

Mary, Queen of all saints . . .

Mary, Queen of heaven and earth . . .

Mary, dispenser of God's graces . . .

Mary, pledge of salvation for those who invoke you . . .

Mary, whose name inspires confidence . . .

Mary, whose hand is always full of blessings . . .

Mary, reflection of Jesus' heart . . .

Mary, model of faith and humility, *pray for our dead*.

Mary, model of interior life . . .

Mary, model of submission to God's will . . .

Mary, model of all virtues . . .

Mary, honor of mankind . . .

Mary, who watches over us in all our needs . . .

Mary, who snatched away the infant Jesus from Herod's fury . . .

Mary, who shared the sufferings of the Redeemer of mankind . . .

Mary, who followed Jesus up to Calvary . . .

Mary, who offered Jesus for our salvation . . .

Mary, whose heart was pierced by a sword . . .

Virgin full of compassion . . .

Mediatrix of peace between God and men . . .

Our advocate near God . . .

Source of life, *pray for our dead*.
Safety of orphans . . .
Haven of sinners . . .
Help of the dying . . .
Hope of the desperate . . .
Heaven's gate . . .
Providence of the unfortunate . . .
Consolation of the afflicted . . .
Our Lady of hope . . .
Our Lady of Montligeon . . .

Holy Mother of God, come to the aid
    of our dead.
That we may be made worthy of the
    promises of Christ.

Let us pray. Lord, our God, through the
intercession of the Blessed Virgin Mary,
grant forgiveness to the dead, abundant
graces to the living, so that all may be one
day reunited in the eternal joy. Through
Jesus Christ Our Lord. Amen.[5]

Prayer in Honor of
St. Benedict for a Happy Death

Prayer in Honor of St. Benedict for a Happy Death

✸

Once, St. Gertrude reminded St. Benedict of his glorious death. St. Benedict gave St. Gertrude the following assurance: "All who invoke me, remembering the glorious death with which God honored me, shall be assisted by me at their death with such fidelity, that I will place myself where I see the enemy most disposed to attack them. Thus being fortified by my presence, they will escape the snares, which he lays for them and depart happily and peacefully to the enjoyment of eternal beatitude."[6]

O holy Father, St. Benedict, blessed by God both in grace and in name, who while standing in prayer with your hands raised to heaven, did most happily yield your angelic spirit into the hands of your Creator; and has promised zealously to defend against all the snares of the enemy, in the last struggle of death, those who should daily remind you of your glorious departure and your heavenly joys; protect me, I beseech you, O glorious Father, St. Benedict, this day and every day by your holy blessing; that I may never be separated from our blessed Lord, from the society of thyself, and of all the blessed. Through Christ our Lord. Amen.

Prayers of the Rosary

Prayers of the Rosary

❧

The Sign of the Cross

In the name of the Father, and of the Son, and of the Holy Spirit. Amen.

The Apostles' Creed

I believe in God, the Father almighty, creator of heaven and earth. I believe in Jesus Christ, his only Son, our Lord. He was conceived by the power of the Holy Spirit and born of the Virgin Mary. He suffered under Pontius Pilate, was crucified, died, and was buried. He descended to the dead. On the third day he arose again. He ascended into heaven, and is seated at the right hand of the Father. He will come again to judge the living and the dead. I believe in the Holy Spirit, the holy catholic Church, the communion of saints, the forgiveness of sins, the resurrection of the body, and the life everlasting. Amen.[7]

The Our Father

Our Father, who art in heaven, hallowed be Thy name; Thy kingdom come; Thy will be done on earth as it is in heaven. Give us this day our daily bread; and forgive us our trespasses as we forgive those who trespass against us; and lead us not into temptation, but deliver us from evil. Amen.

The Hail Mary

Hail Mary, full of grace; the Lord is with thee; blessed art thou among women, and blessed is the fruit of thy womb, Jesus. Holy Mary, Mother of God, pray for us sinners, now and at the hour of our death. Amen.

The Glory Be

Glory be to the Father, and to the Son, and to the Holy Spirit. As it was in the beginning, is now, and ever shall be, world without end. Amen.

The Fátima Prayer

O my Jesus, forgive us our sins. Save us from the fires of hell. Lead all souls to heaven, especially those who are in most need of Your mercy. (*Prayed after each decade. The version used in this book has been adapted to include the holy souls.*)

The Hail, Holy Queen

Hail, Holy Queen, Mother of Mercy, our life, our sweetness, and our hope! To thee do we cry, poor banished children of Eve; to thee do we send up our sighs, mourning and weeping in this valley of tears! Turn then, most gracious Advocate, thine eyes of mercy toward us, and after this, our exile, show unto us the blessed fruit of thy womb, Jesus. O clement, O loving, O sweet Virgin Mary!

Pray for us, O holy Mother of God.

That we may be made worthy of the promises of Christ.

Closing Prayer

Let us pray: O God, whose only-begotten Son, by His life, death, and resurrection, has purchased for us the reward of eternal life; grant, we beseech Thee, that meditating on these mysteries of the most holy Rosary of the Blessed Virgin Mary, we may imitate what they contain and obtain what they promise. Through the same Christ Our Lord. Amen.

May the divine assistance remain always with us. Amen. And may the souls of the faithful departed, through the mercy of God, rest in peace. Amen.

Queen of the Most Holy Rosary, pray for us!

❧

You are encouraged to say the following optional prayers as part of the Rosary.

Prayer to St. Michael

St. Michael the Archangel, defend us in battle. Be our safeguard against the wickedness and snares of the devil. May God rebuke him, we humbly pray, and do thou, O Prince of the Heavenly Host, by the divine power of God, thrust into hell Satan and all the evils spirits who prowl about the world seeking the ruin of souls. Amen.[8]

Prayer of the Angel

O Most Holy Trinity, Father, Son, and Holy Spirit, I adore Thee profoundly. I offer Thee the most precious Body, Blood, Soul, and Divinity of Jesus Christ, present in all the tabernacles of the world, in reparation for the outrages, sacrileges, and indifference by which He is offended. By the infinite merits of the Sacred Heart of Jesus and the Immaculate Heart of Mary, I beg the conversion of poor sinners. Amen.[9]

The Eternal Rest Prayer

Eternal rest grant unto them, O Lord, and let perpetual light shine upon them. May they rest in peace! Amen.

Prayer for the Dead

Queen of the Rosary, thou didst rejoice in God thy Savior, consenting to be the

Mother of Him who would bring salvation to souls. Thou didst announce His mercy as extending from generation to generation. Thou didst proclaim His kindness to the lowly, His mercy in feeding the hungry, His pity in remembering His servants. Mother of Jesus, appeal to Him, therefore, in behalf of His servants, the souls in Purgatory crying from the depths and hungering for the countenance of God, that they too may rejoice in His salvation.

Queen of the Rosary, thou didst suffer with Jesus in His Passion, accepting the office of Mother of mankind at the foot of the Cross. Behold, Mother, thy children whom He commended to thy care. Behold the souls ransomed with the Blood of thy Son. Behold the just suffering in Purgatory, who ask to be remembered by thee. Mother of mankind, speak to thy Son in behalf of those we commend to thee, that they may be speedily released from pain and admitted to Paradise, to the company of Jesus and thee.

Queen of the Rosary, thou hast been enthroned in heaven, not only for thine own sake, but also for ours. To thy hands has been committed the distribution of favors and graces. Thy power reaches from the Church Triumphant to the Church Militant and the Church Suffering. To thee, then, O Queen of mercy, who dwellest in the heavens, we banished children of Eve lift up our eyes and hearts in behalf of the souls of the departed, that thou look with favor upon them and bring them from captivity into the freedom of glorious Zion.

Queen of the Rosary, help our dear ones who have departed this life; our parents, pastors, relatives, friends, benefactors, associates of the Rosary, and every suffering and deserving soul, that their night of sorrow being ended they may be born to the eternal dawn. Offer for them thy joys, sorrows, glories, that thy prayer may supply for what is lacking in our own, thy holiness for our sinfulness, thy love for our indifference, thy power for our weakness. Win for those whom we have lost, the companionship of angels and saints in dwellings of light and peace; obtain for us that we may rejoin them one day in happiness unending. Amen.[10]

The Fifteen Promises of the Blessed Mother

The Fifteen Promises of the Blessed Mother

🌹

1. To all those who will recite my Rosary devoutly, I promise my special protection and very great graces.

2. Those who will persevere in the recitation of my Rosary shall receive some signal grace.

3. The Rosary shall be a powerful armor against hell; it will destroy vice, decrease sin, and defeat heresy.

4. The Rosary shall make virtue and good works flourish; it will obtain for souls the most abundant divine mercies; it will withdraw the hearts of men from the love of the world and its vanities, and will lift

them to the desire of eternal things. Oh, that souls would sanctify themselves by this means!

5. Those who trust themselves to me through the Rosary shall not perish.

6. Those who will recite my Rosary piously, considering its Mysteries, shall not be overwhelmed by misfortune nor die a bad death. The sinner shall be converted; the just shall grow in grace and become worthy of eternal life.

7. Those truly devoted to my Rosary shall not die without the consolations of the Church, or without grace.

8. Those who will recite my Rosary shall find during their life and at their death the light of God, the fullness of His grace, and shall share in the merits of the blessed.

9. *I will deliver very promptly from purgatory the souls devoted to my Rosary.* (Emphasis added.)

10. The true children of my Rosary shall enjoy great glory in heaven.

11. What you ask through my Rosary, you shall obtain.

12. Those who propagate my Rosary shall obtain through me aid in all their necessities.

13. I have obtained from my Divine Son that all the advocates of the Rosary shall have for intercessors the entire celestial court during their life and at the hour of death.

14. All who recite my Rosary faithfully are all my beloved children, the brothers and sisters of Jesus Christ.

15. Devotion to my Rosary is a special sign of predestination.[11]

Act of Consecration to the Immaculate Heart of Mary

Act of Consecration to the Immaculate Heart of Mary

Virgin Mary, Mother of God and our Mother, to your Immaculate Heart I consecrate myself entirely with all that I am and all that I possess.

Take me under your maternal protection, defend me from danger, help me to overcome temptations which lure me to evil and preserve the purity of my body and my soul.

May your Immaculate Heart be my refuge and the way that leads me to God.

Obtain for me the grace of praying and sacrificing myself for the love of Jesus, for the conversion of sinners and in reparation for the offenses committed against your Immaculate Heart.

Through You and in union with the Heart of your Divine Son, I wish to live for the Most Holy Trinity, in Whom I believe, Whom I adore, I hope and I love. Amen.[12]

Our Lady of Fátima

🌹

(The following is from Sister Lucia's book *'Calls' from the Message of Fátima*, with the Blessed Mother's exhortation to pray the Rosary daily taking place on May 13, 1917.)

The Rosary is the prayer which God, through his Church and Our Lady, has recommended most insistently to us all, as a road to and gateway of salvation: *"Pray the Rosary every day."*[13]

Endnotes

1. Michael Müller, C.SS.R., *The Devotion of the Holy Rosary and the Five Scapulars* (New York: Benzinger Brothers, 1876), p. 166.

2. Rev. L.M. Dooley, S.V.D., *Paradise, God's Guest of Tomorrow* (Washington, N.J.: Ave Maria Press and the Blue Army of Our Lady of Fátima, undated), p. 105.

3. Mary Fabyan Windeatt, *St. John Masias* (Rockford, Ill.: TAN Books, 1972), p. 89.

4. *St. Gertrude* (St. Louis: B. Herder Book Co., undated), p. 136.

5. Adapted from a pamphlet (undated) from the Shrine of Our Lady of Montligeon, Perche, Normandy, France.

6. Edward Van Speybrouck, *Father Paul of Moll* (1824-1896) (Rockford, Ill.: TAN Books, reprint of 1910 edition by the Benedictine Convent of Clyde, Mo.), p. 348.

7. International Consultation on English Texts.

8. Pope Leo XIII (pontificate 1878-1903).

9. The Blue Army of Our Lady of Fátima, Washington, N.J.

10. Father Callan and Father McHugh of the Order of Preachers, *Our Lady's Rosary* (P.J. Kenedy & Sons, 1939), pp. 139-140.

11. Charles V. Lacey, *Rosary Novenas to Our Lady* (Benzinger Brothers, 1926, 1954), pp. 6-7.

12. Attributed to Sister Lucia, from a prayer card distributed by the Blue Army of Our Lady of Fátima, Washington, N.J.

13. Sisters of Mosteiro de Santa Maria and Convento de N.S. do Bom Sucesso, Lisbon, trans. (Still River, Mass.: The Ravengate Press [distributor]; copyright 2001 by Coimbra Carmel & Fátima Shrine), p. 134.

About the Author

With this title, Susan Tassone adds another Our Sunday Visitor book to her list of literary accomplishments. Her first work, *The Way of the Cross for the Holy Souls in Purgatory*, has sold more than 50,000 copies. This was followed by her *Praying in the Presence of Our Lord for the Holy Souls*, which was on the Catholic best sellers list twice; it is one of a number of books in the *Praying in the Presence of Our Lord* series by various authors.

Susan, who holds a master's degree in religious education from Loyola University of Chicago and is a consultant for a major nonprofit philanthropic organization in that city, has had the honor and privilege of being granted two private audiences with His Holiness Pope John Paul II.

To order her other books, please contact Our Sunday Visitor (toll-free: 1-800-348-2440; e-mail: osvbooks@osv.com; website: www.osv.com) and ask for:

The Way of the Cross for the Holy Souls in Purgatory, 0-87973-411-6 (411), paper, 48 pages.

Praying in the Presence of Our Lord for the Holy Souls, 0-87973-921-5 (921), paper, 176 pages.

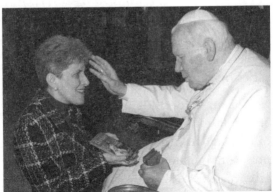

Pope John Paul II bestows his Apostolic Blessing on Susan Tassone's work and her book *Praying in the Presence of Our Lord for the Holy Souls*.

Thirty-Day Devotions for the Holy Souls,
    1-59276-052-X (T103), paper, 160
    pages.

Prayers of Intercession for the Holy Souls (with
    Fr. Benedict J. Groeschel, C.F.R., and
    Fr. John P. Grigus, O.F.M.),
    1-59276-054-6 (M105), audio;
    1-59276-055-4 (M106), CD.

Petitioner's Prayer Notes

❧

Give the joy of offering a Holy Mass for your deceased loved ones and friends.

Consider "Gregorian Masses." Pope St. Gregory the Great popularized this pious practice of offering thirty consecutive Masses for one deceased soul. You can also arrange to have these Masses offered in your will. Contact your local Missions Office for information.

The following pages are dedicated to the souls you wish to list and remember in your daily Rosary: deceased loved ones, deceased consecrated to God (clergy and Religious), deceased friends and benefactors, and deceased whom no one prays for.

DECEASED LOVED ONES

_____

_____

_____

_____

_____

_____

_____

_____

_____

_____

_____

_____

_____

_____

_____

DECEASED CONSECRATED TO GOD
(CLERGY AND RELIGIOUS)

_____

_____

_____

_____

_____

_____

_____

_____

_____

_____

_____

_____

_____

Deceased Friends and Benefactors

_____

_____

_____

_____

_____

_____

_____

_____

_____

_____

_____

_____

_____

_____

_____

_____

_____

_____

_____

_____

_____

_____

_____

_____

_____

_____

_____

_____

_____

_____

DECEASED WHOM NO ONE PRAYS FOR

_____

_____

_____

_____

_____

_____

_____

_____

_____

_____

_____

_____

_____

_____

Our Sunday Visitor ...
Your Source for Discovering the Riches of the Catholic Faith

Our Sunday Visitor has an extensive line of materials for young children, teens, and adults. Our books, Bibles, pamphlets, CD-ROMs, audios, and videos are available in bookstores worldwide.

To receive a FREE full-line catalog or for more information, call **Our Sunday Visitor** at **1-800-348-2440, ext. 3**. Or write **Our Sunday Visitor /** 200 Noll Plaza / Huntington, IN 46750.

Please send me ___ A catalog
Please send me materials on:
___ Apologetics and catechetics
___ Prayer books
___ The family
___ Reference works
___ Heritage and the saints
___ The parish

Name_____
Address_____Apt._____
City _____ State_____Zip_____
Telephone (   )_____
                                                        A39BBABP

Please send a friend ___ A catalog
Please send a friend materials on:
___ Apologetics and catechetics
___ Prayer books
___ The family
___ Reference works
___ Heritage and the saints
___ The parish

Name_____
Address_____Apt._____
City _____ State_____Zip_____
Telephone (   )_____
                                                        A39BBABP

OurSundayVisitor

200 Noll Plaza, Huntington, IN 46750
Toll free: **1-800-348-2440** • Website: www.osv.com